COUNTRIES OF THE WORLD

Greece

Gareth Stevens Publishing
MILWAUKEE

Written by
YEOH HONG NAM

Edited by
KAREN KWEK

Designed by
LYNN CHIN

Picture research by
SUSAN JANE MANUEL

First published in North America in 1999 by
Gareth Stevens Publishing
1555 North RiverCenter Drive, Suite 201
Milwaukee, Wisconsin 53212 USA

For a free color catalog describing
Gareth Stevens' list of high-quality books
and multimedia programs, call
1-800-542-2595 (USA) or
1-800-461-9120 (CANADA)
Gareth Stevens Publishing's
Fax: (414) 225-0377

© **TIMES EDITIONS PTE LTD 1999**
Originated and designed by
Times Books International
an imprint of Times Editions Pte Ltd
Times Centre, 1 New Industrial Road
Singapore 536196
http://www.timesone.com.sg/te

Library of Congress Cataloging-in-Publication Data
Yeoh, Hong Nam.
Greece / by Yeoh Hong Nam.
p. cm. -- (Countries of the world)
Includes bibliographical references and index.
Summary: An overview of this country of southern Europe including
information on its geography, history, government, lifestyles,
languages, art, food, customs, and current issues.
ISBN 0-8368-2309-5 (lib. bdg.)
1. Greece--Juvenile literature. [1. Greece.] I. Title.
II. Series: Countries of the world (Milwaukee, Wis.)
DF741.Y46   1999
949.5--dc21   98-54221

Printed in Malaysia

1 2 3 4 5 6 7 8 9 03 02 01 00 99

About the author: Yeoh Hong Nam lived
in Austria for twelve years and has traveled
extensively in Europe. A free-lance writer based
in Singapore, he has contributed articles on
culture and lifestyle to many publications.

PICTURE CREDITS

A.N.A. Press Agency: 1, 38, 67
Giulio Andreini: 6, 18, 33 (bottom)
Archive Photos: 14, 17
Camera Press: 15 (center), 15 (bottom), 49,
    76, 78, 79, 83 (top)
Bruce Coleman Collection: 3 (bottom),
    9 (bottom), 10, 60, 70
Sylvia Cordaiy Photo Library: 21, 23
John Elk III Photography: 42, 68
Focus Team: Cover, 30, 41 (top), 61, 69
Greek National Tourism Organization: 66
Sonia Halliday: 32, 45
Blaine Harrington: 4
HBL Network Photo Agency: 3 (center), 5,
    7, 31 (top), 43, 47, 59, 62, 74, 87, 89
Dave G. Houser Stock Photography: 16,
    31 (bottom), 48, 64, 85
The Hutchison Library: 20, 24, 25, 34, 71
The Image Bank: 41 (bottom)
Björn Klingwall: 51
Life File Photo Library: 28
North Wind Picture Archives: 15 (top),
    29, 46
Chip Peterson: 54, 82
Photobank Photolibrary: 3 (top), 26, 35
Pietro Scozzari: 2, 65
Richard Shock/Silver Image Photo
    Agency: 75
David Simson: 37, 80, 81, 84
Still Pictures: 72
Liba Taylor Photography: 57
Tom Till Photography: 8
Times Editions: 55, 90 (both)
Topham Picturepoint: 13, 19 (top), 36, 44,
    52, 53, 63, 71, 77, 83 (bottom)
Travel Ink: 9 (top), 11, 19 (top), 91
Trip Photographic Library: 12, 22, 27,
    33 (top), 39, 40, 50, 56, 58 (both), 73

Digital Scanning by Superskill Graphics Pte Ltd

Contents

AN OVERVIEW OF GREECE

According to Greek legend, Greece was created out of the stones that remained behind when the Creator distributed all the sand in the world through a sieve. In fact, rocky outcrops and spectacular gorges characterize parts of the country, but the Greek landscape is more diverse than the legend suggests. Greece also boasts idyllic beaches, forested lowlands, and fertile river basins. This varied landscape is matched by a rich and complex history. Greek culture draws from ancient civilizations, classical Greece, the Byzantine Empire, and almost four hundred years of Turkish rule. At the crossroad of Europe and the Mediterranean, modern Greece also benefits from strong ties with its neighbors and from membership in the European Union.

Opposite: **Greek soldiers in traditional uniform march among the ruins of the Acropolis in Athens.**

Below: **Women on the island of Kárpathos exchange friendly greetings with tourists.**

THE FLAG OF GREECE

Three flags have represented Greece at different periods in its history: a blue-and-white striped flag, a white cross on a blue background, and a combination of these two designs. The current design was adopted as the sole national flag in 1978. It consists of nine horizontal stripes, alternating blue and white, with a white cross on a blue background in the upper left corner. The cross represents Greek Orthodox Christianity, the official religion of Greece. Blue and white are the national colors of Greece: blue for the sky and sea, and white for the purity of the Greek fight for freedom from Turkish rule in the nineteenth century.

Geography

A Land of Contrasts

Greece, or the Hellenic Republic, has an area of 50,949 square miles (131,958 square kilometers) — approximately the size of England or the state of Alabama in the United States.

The Greek landscape boasts stunning peaks and other dramatic geographic features. Eighty percent of the country is mountainous. On the mainland, mountain ranges run northwest to southeast. River valleys and small basins cut deeply into the highlands, leaving scattered lowlands that make up most of the remaining terrain.

Greece can be divided into three parts: the northern mainland, the southern mainland, and the islands and archipelagos. The northern mainland, which borders Albania, the Former Yugoslav Republic of Macedonia, Bulgaria, and Turkey, connects Greece to the rest of Europe. Southward, the thin isthmus at the end of the Gulf of Corinth anchors Peloponnesus,

Below: **This long, sandy stretch of coast is on the island of Crete, in southern Greece.**

Left: **Idyllic Santorini, a group of five islands in the Aegean Sea, was formed about four thousand years ago in a spectacular volcanic eruption. In parts of the islands, the enormous pressures and high temperatures generated by Earth's movements converted limestone to marble, a material that has greatly influenced Greek architecture and artwork.**

a large peninsula, to the mainland. Although islands make up only about 18 percent of the territory of modern Greece, the sea has always played a profound role in defining the Greek mainland. It cuts so deeply into the land that the only area more than 50 miles (80.5 kilometers) inland is a small, triangular section deep in the heart of the country. Over centuries, the sea has carved bays and inlets along the coasts and shaped arms that reach far out to sea as island arcs and archipelagos.

Volcanoes and Earthquakes

The northeastern part of Greece consists of hard rock formed between 345 million and 225 million years ago. Younger, softer limestone formations make up the remaining parts of the country to the south and west. When the whole region was folded into mountains and valleys during the Tertiary period, between 65 million and 1.7 million years ago, much of the land was fractured and placed under great stress, and volcanic eruptions created new islands. Today, as the plates of Earth's crust shift and collide, volcanic activity continues, and earthquakes frequently shake Greece.

A Mediterranean Climate

The physical geography of Greece regulates the climate, keeping it relatively mild. Mountains in the north attract rain, while sea breezes along the coast make the afternoon sun more tolerable. Summers are hot and dry, with average temperatures of about 80° Fahrenheit (27° Celsius). Occasional heat waves, however, can raise the temperature to an uncomfortable 100° F (38° C).

From late autumn onward until spring, warm, moist winds bring rain and storms that disturb the calm of the Aegean Sea. Rain spells are usually short. Although fairly wet, winter rarely produces temperatures lower than 43° F (6° C). The cold season is characterized by low pressure belts from the North Atlantic that shift southward with the chilly weather. These low pressure belts draw cold air from the Balkan mountains in the north, and the air reaches Greece in the form of the bora, an icy wind named after Boreas, the ancient Greek god of the north wind. In mountainous inland regions, snow lingers well into the spring. On the island of Crete, the highest peaks remain snowcapped throughout the year.

Above: The mountainous northwestern part of the Greek mainland attracts rain, which nourishes plants, such as these yellow wildflowers. Behind them jut spires of welded tuff, rock formations of compacted magma from ancient volcanic eruptions.

Unique Species

The plants and animals of Greece originated in Western Asia or the European Balkans. Over the centuries, through natural selection, some of these migrant species evolved into distinct kinds now found nowhere else.

The lower regions of Greece are covered with evergreen trees and colorful flowers. As the land rises, oak, chestnut, pine, and poplar trees become more abundant. At higher altitudes are coniferous forests, consisting mainly of Grecian firs. Irises, crocuses, and tulips carpet the forest clearings.

Greece has a variety of animals, including wildcats, brown bears, and roe deer in the northern forests. Jackals, wild goats, and porcupines live in the lower, hotter regions. Other animals native to the country include a wide variety of reptiles and fish. Many kinds of birds from northern Europe fly south to spend the winter in Greece.

Above: **Bellflowers grow on the dry, rocky slopes of Mt. Parnassus. The soil in Greece is often less fertile than soil in other parts of western Asia and southern Europe. Many plants in Greece have adapted, by becoming shorter and having thinner leaf coverage than plants in other countries.**

Left: **Once hunted for its fur, the European lynx is now a rare sight in Greece.**

ZÁKINTHOS AND MORE

In recent years, Greece has stepped up efforts to save its endangered animals.

(A Closer Look, page 72)

History

The Ancient Past

The known history of Greece dates back almost four thousand years. At that time, the Minoan civilization that thrived on the island of Crete extended its influence as far as the Greek mainland. In the following centuries, Greek naval and military expeditions ranged the Mediterranean Sea and penetrated areas that make up Russia today. The Trojan War, waged against the city of Troy and famously recounted in Homer's epic *Iliad*, was one of these ancient military campaigns.

Classical Greece

During the classical period (fifth century B.C.), Greece was made up of city-states. Each state, or *polis* (POH-lis), was a small country centered around the city that gave it its name. Ruled by kings, the city-states thrived and, under the leadership of Athens, fought off the Persians in about 500 B.C. This era is known as the Golden Age of Athens, a time when Athenian achievements in the arts and sciences were unrivaled.

GREAT THINKERS

Hippocrates, the father of medicine, and Plato, the founder of Western philosophy, both lived in Athens in the fifth century B.C.
(A Closer Look, page 52)

Below: The ancient ruins of the Minoan palace of Knossos, in Crete, draw tourists from all over the world.

From Macedonia to Byzantine Greece

By about 350 B.C., the city-states, weakened by wars against one another in the fifth century B.C., were conquered by King Philip II of Macedonia, in northern Greece. His son, Alexander the Great, united the states and extended the Greek civilization through Egypt, Persian territories, and as far as northern India. Classical Greek dominance came to an end about two centuries after Alexander's death, when the city-states failed to present a united front against a new power — the Roman Empire. Greece became a province of the expanding Roman Empire in 146 B.C. After the Roman conquest, Greece gradually faded as a great political power, although it remained renowned for its culture.

In A.D. 285, the Roman Empire split in two. The eastern half, including Greece, became known as the Byzantine Empire. It was a melting pot of Greek and Roman civilizations. Inhabitants of the empire called themselves Romans but spoke Greek and remained part of the Greek Orthodox Church. In A.D. 330, the Roman emperor Constantine made Byzantium the eastern capital and renamed the city Constantinople (now Istanbul, Turkey).

Above: **The architecture of modern Athens bears the imprint of past empires. An Ionic column dating from the classical period can be seen in the foreground. In the middle stands the Byzantine church of Agia Aikaterini.**

ALEXANDER THE GREAT

Alexander the Great united the Greek city-states and extended his empire to northern India.
(A Closer Look, page 44)

The Fourth Crusade and Ottoman Rule

In 1204, Constantinople was ravaged by the Fourth Crusade, part of a series of European military expeditions directed against Muslim control of Jerusalem between the eleventh and thirteenth centuries. Western powers divided up the Byzantine Empire and occupied parts of Greece. In 1453, Constantinople fell to the Ottoman Empire, a Turkish kingdom founded in 1300 in Anatolia (part of Turkey today). Although the Muslim Turks were tolerant of other religions, they did not rule fairly, and oppression was common. After nearly four hundred years of struggle and many unsuccessful uprisings against the Ottomans, Greek nationalists launched a rebellion in 1821. War continued until the Turkish sultan, Mahmud II, finally recognized Greek independence in 1829.

Troubled Years

The post-independence years were filled with political unrest. In 1831, the assassination of the first Greek president, Count Ioannis Kapodistrias, plunged the entire country into civil war. Frequent changes in government followed. In 1912, however, as war raged through the Balkans, Italy attacked the Ottoman Empire, and Greece found the military strength to seize Macedonia, Crete, Epirus, and the Eastern Aegean islands from the Ottomans, doubling the size and population of Greece. Riding on the wave of revived nationalist hopes, Greek prime minister EleSthérios Venizélos campaigned against Greek King Constantine I for Greece to enter World War I. Greece joined the war in 1917 but gained no new territory. Political instability and general discontent brought a new prime minister, Ioánnis Metaxas, to power. Metaxas persuaded the king to dissolve the parliament. The Metaxas dictatorship lasted from 1936 to 1941.

Italian and German invasions plunged the country into further turmoil during World War II, but Greece's defeat of the Italians and its heroic resistance against the Nazis drew the praise of the free world.

WORLD WAR II

In 1940, Italian dictator Benito Mussolini sent his troops into Greece. The Italians were forced back into Albania by the extremely effective Greek partisans. In 1941, however, German dictator Adolf Hitler conquered the Balkans, including Greece. Greeks fled to the hills in fierce resistance, but the German army occupied Greece until 1944.

Below: German and Italian troops stage a victory parade in Athens in 1941.

The Return to Democracy

Defeated by Britain, France, the U.S.S.R., and the United States, German forces withdrew from Greece in 1945, leaving behind a country on the brink of civil war as communist groups struggled for power. The United States intervened, on behalf of conservative Greek leaders, to defeat Greek communist guerillas in 1949. For the next twenty years, the U.S. government supported Greece with money and arms to combat the spread of communism.

On April 21, 1967, the Greek military, led by Colonel George Papadopoulos, seized power. The junta (the government formed by the military after the coup) became known as "the colonels." They ruled by force, ignoring the demands of modern Greece. In 1973, the world economy went into recession, causing greater discontent in Greece. On July 24, 1974, the junta collapsed, and Constantine Karamanlis, a conservative politician and former Greek prime minister, returned from self-exile in France to restore democracy. Greece abolished the monarchy through a democratic referendum in December 1974.

Below: **Constantine Karamanlis (1907–1998) became prime minister of Greece in 1955. After losing the 1963 election to George Papandreou, he established himself in Paris, returning to Greece in 1974, when the junta collapsed. Karamanlis played an influential role in Greek politics throughout the 1970s and 1980s, and was twice elected president, in 1980 and 1990.**

Solon (c. 630–530 B.C.)

"I freed those who suffered shameful slavery here and trembled at their masters' whims," wrote Athenian statesman Solon, in a poem describing his abolition of slavery in Athens. One of the Seven Wise Men of Greece, Solon fought poverty and provided his countrymen with a balanced constitution and a humane code of laws, establishing the stable foundation on which Athens' later power was built.

Solon

Pericles (c. 495–429 B.C.)

Pericles studied music and philosophy in his youth and gradually rose to assume leadership of the democratic faction in Athens. He established a network of Athenian settlements, strengthening Athenian political control over a wide region during his lifetime. Pericles also commissioned the building of the Parthenon in 447 B.C.

Andreas Papandreou (1919–1996)

Andreas Papandreou was born in Khíos. He was the son of George Papandreou, three-time prime minister of Greece. Andreas Papandreou left Greece when the colonels took over in 1967. When the junta collapsed, he returned and founded his own party, the Panhellenic Socialist Movement (PASOK). The party won a landslide election victory in 1981, and Papandreou became prime minister. He retired from politics in 1996.

Andreas Papandreou

Melina Mercouri (1925–1994)

Melina Mercouri's first career was as an actor. When the junta seized power in 1967, however, she traveled in Europe and North America, inciting public opinion against the takeover. She was so successful that the Greek government revoked her citizenship. When Andreas Papandreou won the general election in 1981, he appointed Mercouri minister of culture. The arts thrived under Mercouri. She is best remembered for asking the British government to return the Elgin Marbles to Greece. The Elgin Marbles were Greek sculptures and architectural details removed from the Parthenon in the early nineteenth century by Thomas Bruce, the seventh earl of Elgin. Melina Mercouri died in New York in 1994.

Melina Mercouri

Government and the Economy

Greece is a presidential republic. A president is the head of state. The foundation for the present Greek constitution was laid after the collapse of the colonels' junta in 1974. From 1974 until 1986, the president had considerable power. Today, however, the president is elected by parliament to a five-year term by parliament and has only ceremonial powers. He or she may serve a maximum of two terms. Real power of government rests with parliament, called the *vouli* (VOO-li), and with a prime minister, the leader of the majority party. Parliament consists of 300 deputies elected to four-year terms through a compulsory secret ballot. With parliamentary consent, the president may declare war and conclude agreements of peace, alliance, and participation in international organizations. The current president is Konstantinos Stephanopoulos, and the prime minister is Costas Simitis.

BIRTHPLACE OF DEMOCRACY

Democracy, or rule by the people, was born in classical Greece. Athenian democracy allowed people to express their views in the *ekklesia* (ek-KLEE-see-ah), or popular assembly, a gathering of debaters.

Below: The parliament building in Athens. In the foreground is Constitution Square.

Above: **Greek soldiers guard an air base.**

Greece is divided into nine mainland regions and four island regions. These thirteen regions are further divided into fifty-one departments run by elected prefects. The Panhellenic Socialist Movement (PASOK) and the New Democratic Party dominate Greek politics. PASOK controlled parliament from 1981 through 1989. In 1990, PASOK lost the election to the New Democratic Party but regained power in the 1993 election.

Judicial System and Defense

The Greek Supreme Court handles criminal and civil cases, and the Council of State deals with administrative law. The Court of State Auditors oversees financial matters. As a check on the government, the heads of these three courts also sit on a Special Supreme Tribunal, which handles constitutional issues and ensures that parliamentary elections and referenda are valid.

Of all countries in the North Atlantic Treaty Organization (NATO), Greece spends the largest proportion of its budget (about 6 percent) on defense. Military service is compulsory for Greek men, and women may serve if they wish.

CYPRUS

Historically, Greek influence in Cyprus, a Mediterranean island south of Turkey, has always been strong, and about 80 percent of its population is ethnically Greek. Cyprus gained independence from the British in 1960. In 1974, however, Turkish forces invaded northern Cyprus, dividing the island into opposing Turkish-controlled and Greek-controlled halves. This dispute over the island is still unresolved today.

(A Closer Look, page 48)

Economic Development

Despite economic progress in recent years and reducing inflation and public deficits, Greece still lags behind the more advanced countries in the European Union. Its main problems are a scarcity of natural resources and limited industrialization. The country's major sources of income are shipping, tourism, and remittances by Greeks living and working overseas, often in the United States. By January 1, 2001, Greece will join other European countries in using a single European currency, called the Euro.

Employment

Traditionally, most Greeks have been self-employed, preferring to work in small cottage industries rather than for large corporations. In the past, Greece was an agricultural country. Now, however, service is the fastest growing sector of the Greek economy, accounting for over 60 percent of national income.

The number of Greeks working overseas is declining as the need for immigrant labor in other countries decreases. Recent improvements in living standards are keeping most Greeks at home, making large-scale emigration a thing of the past.

Above: **A harvester in Crete loads containers of grapes into a cart. Greece is renowned for a variety of delicious fruit, grown for both local and overseas markets.**

Natural Resources, Industry, and Trade

Greece's most significant natural resources are reserves of bauxite, which is used to make aluminum, and lignite, a low-grade form of coal. Oil lies under the Aegean Sea, near the island of Thásos, but it cannot be mined until a dispute with Turkey is settled. Since the 1950s, increasing migration from the countryside to the cities has caused decreased agricultural efficiency. Today, the most fertile farmland in Greece is on the plains of Thessaly and in Eastern Macedonia and Thrace. Here, grain and sugar beets are grown for food, while tobacco and cotton are grown for export. Other significant agricultural products include olives, grapes, melons, peaches, tomatoes, and oranges. The fishing industry, once a mainstay of the Greek economy, has been declining in recent years because modern fishing methods have led to overfishing.

Membership in the European Union (EU) is now helping to boost the Greek economy. Most Greek trade is with fellow members of the EU, especially Germany and Italy. The country's major exports are steel, aluminum, cement, food, livestock, and petroleum-based products.

OLIVES AND OLIVE OIL

Ancient Greeks considered the olive a gift from the gods. Today, its marvelous products, exported worldwide, contribute to the Greek economy.
(*A Closer Look, page 60*)

Left: **Cars and trucks are being unloaded from a ship at the port of Préveza in Epirus. The shipping industry is a growing and vibrant part of the Greek economy. Together with tourism, shipping contributes about 10 percent of the country's gross national product.**

CONQUERING THE SEAS

Greek ships have been traveling the Mediterranean Sea since 2000 B.C. Today, the Greek-owned shipping network is the largest in the world.
(*A Closer Look, page 46*)

People and Lifestyle

Greeks call themselves Hellenes. They have lived on the same land for about three thousand years. Despite centuries of occupation by the Roman and Ottoman empires, as well as an invasion by the Slavs, Greeks have maintained their language, traditions, and identity.

Hellenes

Modern Greece is an ethnically homogeneous nation, with only tiny minorities of Turks, Vlachs, Slavs, Albanians, Jews, and Gypsies. During the four hundred years of Turkish rule, different nationalities and ethnic groups from Turkey and Europe settled in Greece. Since independence in the nineteenth century, however, the population has returned to its near-homogeneous composition. Today, about 98 percent of the Greek population belongs to the Greek Orthodox Church. Only about 2 percent are ethnic minorities.

Below: **A Greek farmer enjoys the company of his two grandchildren.**

Muslims

The only sizeable minority in Greece is Muslim. The Muslim community is concentrated in the northeastern part of the country and numbers close to 120,000 people, or 1 percent of the population. About half of the Muslims are of Turkish descent. Muslims in Greece are ensured representation by four elected members of parliament.

Albanians

In the twelfth century, Albanians from Eastern Europe were brought into Greece to settle underpopulated areas. They formed communities in Thessaly, Attica, and Peloponnesus. A fierce, warlike people, they also served the Byzantine emperors as soldiers, sometimes ruling small territories for their overlords. The traces Albanians left to historians are mainly in names of places or words in local dialects. Today, they are Greek Orthodox Christians who consider themselves Greek. Recently, however, Greece provided shelter and employment to some 300,000 Albanian refugees who entered Greece as legal or illegal workers.

Above: **A Gypsy shopkeeper in Kérkira (Corfu) plays the guitar. Greece has a tiny, scattered Gypsy population. Once nomadic entertainers, fortune-tellers, and horse traders, most Gypsies are now permanently settled.**

Family Ties

The close-knit structure of the Greek family has historical roots. Until the twentieth century, most Greeks lived in the countryside. The rugged nature of the land made travel between neighboring villages difficult, so many village communities kept to themselves. Although advances in transportation and communications have opened up most of Greece to travel, family loyalty remains a strong component of Greek life. Today, urban life is often more independent, but in the Greek social code, families still look after their own before anyone else. This loyalty is evident in small industries and shipping, where many businesses are still family run.

Traditionally, one of the goals of a Greek family was to give their marrying daughters dowries to secure the newlyweds a comfortable life. This custom was prevalent at a time when men worked and women stayed at home to take care of the family. The

Below: This extended family is celebrating Christmas. Holidays are occasions for the whole family to get together.

Above: **This group of Greek men is spending the afternoon chatting and relaxing at a local coffee shop. In conservative communities and families, men and women have separate social circles and pastimes.**

Greek government abolished the dowry system in the early 1980s, so this tradition is rarely practiced today. Also, because many women are financially independent, a dowry is no longer required.

Gender Roles

In the past, gender roles were very distinct in traditional Greek society. A man worked to provide for his family, while his wife stayed at home. Modernization and education have largely changed these roles. As in many countries worldwide, Greek women today enjoy the freedom to choose whether to have a career, a family, or both.

Godparents

A family in Greece often extends beyond blood relatives. At birth, every child has a *nonos* (noh-NOS), or godparent, chosen from an unrelated family. The godparent bears a spiritual responsibility for the child and may provide financial or emotional support as the child grows up. The relationship between godparents and godchildren in Greece is so respected that, under religious law, godchildren must regard the children of their godparents as siblings and are not permitted to marry them.

THE WOMEN OF GREECE

In traditional Greek society, the woman's domain was the home. Today, however, more women are entering the work force.
(A Closer Look, page 70)

An Intellectual Tradition

Greeks have always valued the cultivation of ideas. Many ancient Greeks studied the arts of rhetoric and oratory under the tutelage of famous thinkers of their time. Greek intellectuals also endowed subsequent civilizations with a wealth of knowledge in the fields of medicine, astronomy, mathematics, and philosophy.

Education is still a priority in Greek culture, and, today, Greece boasts a 95 percent literacy rate, one of the highest in the world. All children from the ages of six to twelve must attend primary school, after which students spend three years at a *gymnasium* (jim-NAH-see-um), an institution for students aged thirteen to fifteen, before going on to high school, known as *lyceum* (lee-SEE-um).

Public primary, secondary, and higher education is free, but students frequently supplement regular classes with lessons at private schools. These lessons allow them to improve their English and foreign language skills or to prepare for university entrance examinations. Some Greeks choose to send their children overseas to study.

Above: **Students respond eagerly in a Greek primary school.**

Higher Education

After high school, students face tremendous competition for university places because there are fewer places than there are qualified students. Since the 1960s, changes in attitudes toward higher education have made the shortage even more acute. The path to respectability for young people increasingly leads away from family farms toward secure jobs in the cities. Today, the minimum qualification for a civil service position is a university diploma, and more and more young people are recognizing the need for higher education.

Government efforts to tackle the education shortage problem have achieved some success. Education reforms in the last twenty years have improved the quality of schools and universities. Students have also benefited from exchange programs with institutions in other countries. Since 1960, universities have been established in Ioánnina, Pátrai, Crete, Kérkira, Thessaly, and the Aegean Islands. The oldest universities in Greece are the National Capodistrian University of Athens, established in 1837, the National Technical University of Athens (1836), and the Aristotelian University of Thessaloníki (1925).

Below: **University students take a break between classes.**

Greek Orthodox Christianity

Greek Orthodox Christianity is an important branch of Eastern Orthodoxy, the belief retained by the Byzantine Empire when the Roman Empire split in A.D. 285. The Greek Orthodox Church became independent of Constantinople in 1850, after Greece achieved independence from Turkish rule. Today, the Church is self-governing but still recognizes the Ecumenical Patriarch in Istanbul as its spiritual leader.

The 10 million Greeks faithful to the Greek Orthodox Church live in eighty-one dioceses, or religious districts, run by the bishops of the Church. A synod of all Orthodox bishops makes decisions concerning the Church. Another synod of twelve bishops oversees the day-to-day running of the Church. Both synods are chaired by the Archbishop of Athens and All Greece. Orthodox priests participate actively in community life. They

Above: **The abbott (arms raised) of the Monastery of St. John in Patmos participates in the Niptras (nip-TRAS), or washing, ceremony before Good Friday. The ceremony reenacts Jesus Christ's washing of his disciples' feet before the Last Supper.**

are welcome guests at family celebrations, presiding over important religious ceremonies, such as baptisms, weddings, and funerals.

Lives of Religious Dedication

Monasteries have been a significant part of Greek spiritual life for about a thousand years. Greek Orthodox monks in the Pindus Mountains spend their days in disciplined meditation and contemplation. Anchoritic monks live alone in remote places and have very little contact with other people. Not all monks, however, lead lives of seclusion. Cenobitic monks, who live in a community, share possessions, duties, and meals. Idiorrhythmic monks meet with one another only for feast day celebrations and Sunday services. Otherwise, they observe separate and individual spiritual lifestyles. Today, fewer and fewer young people are drawn to the monastic life.

Minority Religions

Only about 2 percent of the Greek population is not Orthodox. Greek Muslims are concentrated in the Dodecanese Islands and in western Thrace. Small communities of Roman Catholics live on the Aegean islands. Protestants number only a few thousand in Greece, and the once-large Jewish population was greatly diminished by Nazi persecution during World War II.

THE EVIL EYE

Some Greeks believe blue beads can protect loved ones from the alleged curse of the evil eye.
(*A Closer Look, page 50*)

OF GODS AND GODDESSES

Almost everyone has heard of Zeus and his jealous wife, Hera, or of the great beauty of Aphrodite, the goddess of love. These and other tales of deities and humans survive today.
(*A Closer Look, page 58*)

Below: **The Meteora monasteries are perched atop remote, rocky outcrops in the Pindus Mountains of Thessaly.**

Language and Literature

Modern Greek derives from the same idiom used by Homer and other famous Greek writers and poets more than three thousand years ago. Greek was the language of the Gospels and has made a major contribution to all Western languages. When the Byzantine Empire was formed in A.D. 285, Greek was made the official language of the empire in the east. The Greek dialect then in use was *dimotiki* (dee-moh-tee-KEE), or demotic Greek, a form based on ancient Greek and historically spoken by common people.

In the 1830s, Adamantios Korais, a Greek scholar with a passionate interest in the classical Greek heritage, suggested creating a superior Greek language based on classical Greek. This artificial language, *katharévousa* (kah-thah-REH-voo-sah), was easier to learn than classical Greek and believed to be purer than dimotiki. Unfortunately, katharévousa proved much harder to learn than anyone had anticipated! The language never became very popular. In 1975, demotic Greek became the official language, but, because katharévousa appeared in most publications before 1975, modern Greek still contains some of its elements.

THE GREEK ALPHABET

The word *alphabet* comes from *alpha* (AL-fah) and *beta* (VEE-tah), the first two letters of the Greek alphabet.
(*A Closer Look*, page 54)

Below: Signs in Athens are posted in two languages, Greek (yellow) and English (white).

Literature: Ancient . . .

One of the most famous ancient stories in the world was composed by the Greek poet Homer 2,500 to 3,000 years ago. The *Iliad*, an epic that unfolds in thousands of verses, tells of the war between the Greeks and the city of Troy, describing exciting battles and heroic deeds. Homer's second epic, the *Odyssey*, describes the return of the Greek king Odysseus after the war with Troy. Odysseus receives help from some gods, while others try to delay or prevent him from returning to his family in Ithaca. The works of other Greek scholars and writers also survive as classics today. Ancient Greek dramatists such as Sophocles and Euripides lived more than 2,400 years ago, during a period that also produced the great historians Herodotus and Thucydides.

. . . and Contemporary

Writers such as George Seferis, Odysseus Elytis, and Níkos Kazantzakís popularized twentieth-century Greek literature. Seferis and Elytis were each awarded the Nobel Prize for literature in 1963 and 1979 respectively. Kazantzakís produced a wide variety of works. His novels *Zorba the Greek* and *The Last Temptation of Christ* have both been made into American films.

POETRY

Before writing was invented, stories were shared by word of mouth. Bards, or professional storytellers, entertained their audiences with tales from the heroic past. Rhythm and rhyme helped these entertainers remember their stories. Later, all ancient Greek plays and even political and legal texts were written in verse. The legislator Solon addressed his reforms to the Athenians as poems for all to read and remember.

Arts

Among the marvels of human history, the arts of ancient Greece encompass four main periods: geometric (1100–700 B.C.), archaic (700–500 B.C.), classical (500–323 B.C.), and Hellenistic (from 323 B.C.).

Architectural Wonders

During the geometric period, builders used simple, symmetrical designs. Only the ruins of ancient temples, such as those in Crete and Sparta, survive from this period.

From 650 B.C., in the archaic period, the Greeks started trading with the Egyptians. They were impressed with the massive stone columns and carvings they saw in Egypt and took these architectural and artistic ideas home with them. Human figures, which were carved in stone and used to decorate buildings, became more lifelike and three-dimensional than their geometric predecessors. It was also in the archaic period that marble became

THE PARTHENON

Built in the fifth century B.C., the Parthenon remains one of the most famous architectural treasures of Western civilization.
(A Closer Look, page 65)

Below: **The temple of Delphi was the site of the Oracle of Apollo. Ancient Greeks consulted the oracle on private matters as well as state affairs.**

a favored building material. This durable medium captured the extraordinary work of the Greek masters for future generations.

During the classical period, the Greek city-states, fiercely jealous of each other, lavished the finest paintings and sculpture on splendid architecture in efforts to outdo one another. Classical builders favored temples in the Doric, Ionic, and Corinthian orders, architectural styles characterized by distinct proportions, column styles, and other details. Probably the most famous example of a Doric temple is the Parthenon in Athens. Elements of Asian art and architecture were incorporated with traditional styles during the Hellenistic period, after the conquests of Alexander the Great.

Folk Art and Crafts

Pottery developed on Greek islands and the southern part of the mainland thousands of years ago. Other regions of Greece became known for their excellent metalwork. Today, terra cotta pottery, leather sandals, and replicas of ancient artifacts are sold in street stalls throughout Greece.

From Religious Icons to Contemporary Landscapes

The earliest Greek paintings survive today only in faded fragments, but art historians have recovered and preserved religious icons from the Byzantine period. In A.D. 843, when a law forbidding artists to depict human figures in religious scenes was abolished, Greek artists joyfully returned to their love of portraying the human body and religious themes. Many icons were of Jesus Christ alone or the Virgin Mary with the baby Jesus. Often framed against a gold-colored background, the subject was emphasized by unrealistic or distorted perspective. A wide variety of other painting styles flourished on the Ionian Islands, which were free from Turkish occupation during the fifteenth to nineteenth centuries. Ionian artists were influenced by Venetian painters and the Italian Renaissance, a period of great artistic flowering. Today, twentieth-century Greek painters, such as Odysseus Phocas and Spyros Vikatos, are famous for their landscapes and portraits.

Above: **The walls of a church in Cyprus are adorned with a twelfth-century mural depicting biblical characters.**

Music and Dance

No Greek celebration is complete without music, singing, and dancing. Groups of guitarists and drummers enliven the atmosphere at traditional celebrations, and people sing folk songs to mark every occasion, from weddings to the changing of seasons. Dancers in colorful costumes display their skills during festivals and on special occasions, such as Christmas and Easter. Greeks have hundreds of folk dances, from the solemn and dignified to the lively and happy. Today, Western-influenced Greek pop and rock bands play music that no doubt perplexes conservative Greeks!

Other Pastimes

Greeks are master craftspeople; many enjoy pottery and sculpture. Reading is another popular pastime. Greece boasts a strong literacy tradition, and many Greeks are amateur writers and poets.

Above: **Holding hands, Greek folk dancers usually form a line or an open circle.**

Left: **Soccer player Neophytus Larkou (right) of Cyprus competes with Wales' Ryan Giggs for the ball in a World Cup qualifying match in Cardiff, Wales, in 1993.**

Sporting Traditions

Home to the Olympic Games, Greece is a nation of amateur and professional athletes. Wrestling was a favorite sport in ancient times, and, today, Greece lends its name to the Olympic art of Greco-Roman wrestling. Weightlifting and sailing have produced Olympic medalists for Greece.

The national sport of Greece is *podosphero* (poh-DOHS-fay-roh), or soccer, and local teams command an almost fanatical allegiance from supporters. Local soccer stars attain heroic status, and many a young man's dream is to make it big on the soccer field. Greece has an eighteen-team soccer league. League games are played on Sundays.

Basketball also has a big following in Greece. Since the Greek team won the European basketball championship in 1987, the sport has been growing in popularity.

A Love of the Outdoors

Greeks enjoy a wide variety of outdoor sports and games, including skiing, hunting, and automobile racing. Several ski centers in the snowcapped mountains of central Greece cater to ski enthusiasts. The rural history of the country might explain the appeal of hunting. In the past, shooting small game was a useful way of adding meat to a diet that consisted mainly of vegetables and fish. Today, however, as cities encroach on natural animal habitats, environmental lobbyists criticize hunters for their destructive activities. To protect endangered species, the government has established a number of wildlife sanctuaries, where animals can live and raise their young in safety.

Beachside Fun and Water Sports

With their spectacular bays, inlets, and clear, blue seas, the Greek islands are perfect for water sports of all kinds. They attract tourists from all over the world, as well as Greeks from the mainland. Greeks enjoy fishing, sailing, waterskiing, boating, rowing, or just sunbathing on the white, sandy beaches. Children learn to swim at a very young age. The clear waters off the island coasts also provide the perfect opportunity for swimmers and divers to observe marine life up close.

THE OLYMPIC GAMES

The Olympic Games began in ancient Greece and were revived in 1896 in Athens by Frenchman Baron Pierre de Coubertin.
(*A Closer Look, page 62*)

Below: Hungry swimmers on the island of Kérkira allow a restaurant owner to entice them with the special of the day, fresh lobsters. The Greek islands are an ideal setting for a variety of outdoor activities, including swimming and fishing.

Pascha

The most important day in the Greek Orthodox calendar is *Pascha* (PAHS-kah), or Easter, which commemorates Jesus Christ's resurrection on the third day after his crucifixion and death. The carnival season begins about three weeks before Lent, the forty-day period of fasting that precedes Easter. Once Lent begins, there is no more revelry, and many Greeks fast by giving up meat and dairy products. Good Friday is marked by a total fast. At midnight on Holy Saturday, processions leave from churches in darkness, reenacting the search for Christ's body. When the participants return, a priest lights the candle held by each believer, symbolizing the passing on of the holy flame. With the announcement that "Christ has risen," everyone enters the church for a special service to honor the miracle of Easter. They take their candles home after the service to represent carrying home the spirit of Easter. At dawn on Easter Sunday, wearing their finest festive clothes, they attend the Easter service. The rest of the day is spent feasting and having fun.

Below: **Women on the island of Kárpathos celebrate Easter in elaborate traditional dress.**

Celebrating Independence

In a calendar dominated by religious holidays, Independence Day holds special significance for Greeks because it marks the end of almost four centuries of Turkish domination. In 1829, after an eight-year struggle to liberate their country, Greeks finally won their independence. Greek Independence Day, March 25, commemorates this courageous battle and victory. Greeks throughout the country observe this national holiday with spectacular fireworks displays.

Saying "No"

October 28, or Ochi Day, is a national holiday with great historical significance. During World War II, when Greek prime minister Ioánnis Metaxas was asked to let Italian troops occupy Greece, Metaxas replied with a firm *ochi* (o-HEE), meaning "no." Greek soldiers defeated the Italian forces that invaded Greece in 1940. Metaxas' staunch refusal represented Greek pride and a spirit of independence.

Above: **Greek student groups and military units take part in an Ochi Day parade.**

NAMES AND NAME DAYS

Instead of celebrating birthdays, most Greeks celebrate name days, feast days of their namesake saints.
(*A Closer Look, page 56*)

Food

Greece has been perfecting the art of cooking for more than four thousand years. In 330 B.C., Archestratos wrote the first cookbook in history. Since then, Greek cuisine has been evolving, absorbing ideas and flavors from the Middle East and Western Europe.

There are four keys to Greek cooking: fresh ingredients; the careful use of herbs and spices; olive oil; and good, honest simplicity. Indeed, Greek food is so naturally appetizing and tasty that it requires little or no artificial enhancers. Visitors are often surprised by the fresh taste and juicy goodness of local vegetables. The secret is the sunny Mediterranean climate, which allows vegetables and herbs to grow and ripen naturally in the fields. Unlike other parts of Europe and North America, greenhouses are unnecessary.

DRINKS

Greek coffee, or *kafedaki* (kah-fay-DHAH-kee), is strong and dark. The Greek national drink is *ouzo* (OO-zoh), a strong, clear liquor with an anise and licorice flavor. *Retsina* (ret-SEE-nah) is a Greek wine with the distinct flavor of resin.

Below: **An extended family enjoys a feast on Easter Sunday.**

SWEET TREATS

Perhaps the most delicious cakes and pastries are found in the bakeries of Greece.
(*A Closer Look, page 68*)

Left: Souvlaki, or barbecued lamb kebabs, is a favorite Greek food.

Favorite dishes in Greece include seafood and lamb. Combined with the flavors of oregano, thyme, spearmint, or rosemary, these foods taste truly heavenly. Fresh Mediterranean seafood is best enjoyed grilled over an open wood fire. *Kalamari* (ka-lah-MAH-ree), or squid, is a well-known delight. Another famous treat is a long skewer of meat and vegetables cooked over an open fire. *Souvlaki* (soov-LAH-kee) are barbecued lamb kebabs. Mixed into salads or for a snack, cheeses made from goat's or sheep's milk are also popular.

Dessert often consists of fresh fruit or delicious pastries. Grapes, apricots, peaches, cherries, melons, and pears are all part of the bounty of Greece.

The Philosophy of Eating Well

Mealtimes are very important to Greeks. The customs of hospitality and sharing food with friends are vital parts of Greek culture. A Greek host or hostess might spend days preparing food for guests. Even amateur cooks are respected among friends. For Greeks, keeping a good house means being able to prepare good food and making guests feel welcome.

Below: A market in Iráklion, Crete, sells fresh, choice vegetables. Tomatoes, eggplant, lettuce, carrots, onions, parsley, and garlic — Greeks love them all.

41

A CLOSER LOOK AT GREECE

Greeks are the proud heirs of an ancient civilization, and the influence of the country's eventful past is felt all around the world. Greeks were among the earliest seafarers in the Mediterranean, shaping a maritime tradition that continues today with Greek domination of global shipping networks. The ideas of great men such as Plato and Hippocrates laid the foundation for Western philosophy and medicine. The Greeks also gave the world an enduring mythology, one of the earliest alphabets ever invented, and the Olympic Games, the most prestigious international sporting event today.

Opposite: **Residents and tourists mingle in a street in Kérkira.**

Below: **News vendors in Greece cater to a nation of avid readers.**

Modern Greeks are something of a paradox. Some adhere to traditional superstitions that might surprise visitors and invite criticism for being "unscientific." Yet Greek experts boast several advances in research, especially in environmental conservation. Greek women are redefining traditional gender roles and carving a niche for themselves in the work force. From the delights of Greek pastries and desserts to ongoing ethnic tensions in Cyprus, this section examines aspects of a rich culture born of two worlds, ancient and modern.

Alexander the Great

At the age of thirty-three, Alexander the Great, one of the greatest generals in history, lay on his deathbed. His kingdom and Greek influence stretched from Macedonia, in northern Greece, into Persia, Egypt, Syria, and Asia. Asked who should succeed him, Alexander's cryptic reply was, reportedly, "The best one." His death marked the passing of one of the most successful and legendary episodes in Greek history. Stories about the life and military conquests of Alexander the Great grew to mythic proportions over the centuries.

Alexander's first military victory came at the tender age of sixteen, over the Maedi, a people from Thrace. In 338 B.C., he defeated the allied Greek states, and, two years later, when his father was assassinated, Alexander succeeded him as king. After killing his father's suspected murderers and all potential rivals to the throne, Alexander set out to conquer the rest of Greece, Persia, and Asia.

Thebes, Athens, and other allied Greek states allowed Macedonian forces to set up garrisons in their cities after Alexander brutally conquered Thebes. His next move was against

Below: **Born in 356 B.C. at Pella, in Macedonia, to Philip II and his queen, Olympias, Alexander the Great (left) studied philosophy, medicine, and science under the tutelage of the Greek philosopher Aristotle.**

Left: Alexander the Great was an inspiring leader in battle. The backbone of his formidable army was the cavalry, which consisted of about five thousand armed horsemen. The infantry numbered about nine thousand, moving against the enemy in a phalanx, a relentless wall of foot soldiers bearing shields and long spears.

Persia, the Greeks' fiercest enemy. The Persian empire was broken after a series of battles. Alexander's army left in its wake the ravaged city of Tyre and a subdued Babylon. After King Darius of Persia died, Alexander's forces advanced throughout Persia and on into India. Called "invincible" by a priestess of the Oracle at Delphi, Alexander began to believe in his own divinity, decreeing that his subjects recognize and pay tribute to him as a god.

The years of war, however, took their toll on Alexander's army. In the northern hills of India, the men, wounded and tired of battle, discouraged their leader from penetrating farther. Alexander agreed to retreat, but he never made it back to Macedonia. He fell ill after extended feasting and drinking and died on June 13, 323 B.C.

THE END OF AN EMPIRE

After Alexander the Great died, each of his generals declared himself king, and Alexander's empire subsequently crumbled. His legacy, however, was the spread of the Greek economy, language, and culture throughout a vast region, paving the way for a Greek consciousness and identity much later.

Conquering the Seas

Because so much of Greece is relatively close to the sea, maritime activities from fishing to commerce have always played an important part in Greek lifestyle. Today, Greek businessmen and shipping magnates own and operate the largest fleet of merchant ships in the world, with a network of shipping routes that crisscrosses the globe.

Rowing Galleys and Sailing Ships

The history of Greek shipping dates back as far as 2000 B.C., when seagoing vessels first appeared in the Mediterranean. The Minoan civilization on Crete built its first ships out of wooden planks and logs. Gradually, they discovered that certain functions called for certain kinds of vessels. Ships used in war, for example, required greater speed, while trading ships required greater stability and cargo volume. The first ships in the Mediterranean were all propelled by oars and rowers. The only way to increase the speed of early warships was to have more rowers on board.

Below: **Odysseus defies the Cyclops, a mythical giant with one eye, in Homer's epic, the *Odyssey*. Early ships in the Mediterranean probably resembled the one shown here.**

46

By the time of classical Greece, rowing galleys had up to three tiers of rowers.

Meanwhile, a small revolution in shipbuilding was taking place in the northern hemisphere, where wind directions changed frequently. Sails were invented to harness the power of the wind. As more complex sails were developed, Greek sailing vessels dominated commerce in the Aegean, building a lucrative inter-island trade. Greek merchants continued to trade on the seas throughout the fourteenth century. The next four hundred years, however, saw many marine battles and the looting of Greek islands and coastal areas by the Ottoman Turks.

In the nineteenth and twentieth centuries, Greek merchants entered and consolidated their hold on international shipping. During World War I, they expanded into the Atlantic. By the end of World War II, they were exploiting business opportunities in the Pacific and Indian oceans. Increasing emigration created pockets of Greek communities throughout the world. Wherever Greeks settled, they retained their cultural identity and ties to their homeland. Although their ships flew the flags of individual ports of origin from London to Singapore, a shared "Greekness" preserved an international network of Greek connections.

Above: **Tourists arrive in the Cyclades Islands on a Greek cruise liner. Today, Greece operates an extensive inter-island cruise network. Greek-owned vessels also form the largest merchant fleet in the world.**

Cyprus

After Sicily and Sardinia, Cyprus is the third largest island in the Mediterranean. Basking in a warm climate with mild winters, it is home to an abundance of plant and animal life.

Cyprus has a long historical and mythological association with Greece; the Greek goddess Aphrodite is said to have emerged from the sea near the scenic southwestern coast of Cyprus. Despite traditional Greek influence, however, its geographical location just south of Turkey has resulted in longstanding political conflict between Greece and Turkey.

A Turbulent History

The first Greek settlers arrived on the island in 1200 B.C. and gradually built kingdoms throughout Cyprus. Although the island was later conquered by a series of different civilizations, Greek influence remained, and the majority of the population continued to speak the Greek language.

Left: **Petra tou Rominou, on the southwestern coast of Cyprus, is said to be the birthplace of the Greek goddess Aphrodite.**

During the fifteenth century, when the Ottoman Empire based in Turkey expanded, Turks joined the island population, and tension rose between the Greek majority and the Turkish minority. British occupation in 1898 held the growing conflict in check, but when the island gained independence from Britain in August 1960, the two ethnic groups failed to settle their differences peacefully. Fighting broke out in 1963, and the following year, both parties approached the United Nations for help in mediating the conflict. Although the United Nations stationed a multi-national force known as the U.N. Peace-Keeping Force on the island, Turkish troops invaded Cyprus and, in 1974, occupied the northern part of the island. Turkish Cypriots established a separate state recognized only by Turkey, the Turkish Republic of Northern Cyprus.

Today, Cyprus remains a divided and contested territory. Following a remarkable economic recovery from the setback of the partition, it now supports a thriving tourist industry despite its political difficulties. Growing capitalism in Eastern Europe has also increased the volume of trade passing through the island. Talks to integrate Cyprus into the European Union began in 1996.

Above: **Members of the U.N. Peace-Keeping Force patrol the streets of Cyprus. Turkish refusal to withdraw from northern Cyprus is a stumbling block to negotiations directed toward integrating Cyprus with the European Union.**

The Evil Eye

Whenever something goes wrong, superstitious Greeks know what to blame. Belief in the evil eye, a mysterious force thought to be responsible for misfortune, illness, and even death, probably originated in ancient Greece and Rome. This superstition is prevalent in many cultures today. In Greece, people from all walks of life, from fishermen to university professors, recognize its signs, a heavy head and a feeling of weakness. The majority of Greeks, however, only humorously entertain the idea.

Mysterious Causes

The curse of the evil eye is not always cast out of malice. Some believe it can occur involuntarily when someone praises or admires something precious. For this reason, people are cautious with their praise of newborn infants, not wishing to bring on the curse.

Over the centuries, Greeks devised methods of protection against the evil eye. Some believe that wearing necklaces of blue

Left: Centuries ago, many people believed that "eyes" painted on boats and ships would keep away monsters and evil spirits encountered at sea. This superstition might have fueled belief in the evil eye.

beads or pendants patterned to resemble eyes will ward off evil. Adults wear their protective beads on the same chain as their crucifixes, while children wear a small image of the Virgin Mary pinned to their clothes.

Above: **This little girl is wearing a pendant designed to ward off the evil eye.**

Removing the Curse

When someone is believed to be under the curse of the evil eye, the cure is usually undertaken by an old woman with a reputation for wisdom. Typically, she takes a glass of water and makes the sign of the cross over it three times. Then, she recites a secret passage from the Bible three times, while dripping three droplets of olive oil into the water. If the oil droplets form globules in the water, the person is judged unaffected by the evil eye. Droplets that disperse, however, are a sign that is considered both proof and cure of the curse. Believers say that the symptoms of the curse disappear once the cure takes effect. Other than attributing this change to the power of mind over body, science has no explanation for the phenomenon. Is the evil eye real? You be the judge.

Great Thinkers

Hippocrates

Experts believe Hippocrates lived from about 460 to about 377 B.C. and might have been a contemporary of the famous Greek philosopher Socrates.

Much of what we know today about Hippocrates comes from the writings of philosophers, such as Plato and Aristotle. According to Plato, Hippocrates enjoyed a far-reaching reputation as a doctor. Aristotle called him "the Great Physician." Hippocrates' contributions to Greek medicine range from anatomy to studies of drugs and cures for diseases. His own works, the Hippocratic Collection, present his concept of the human body as a system whose parts function within a whole. From the Hippocratic Collection, we also know that ancient Greek doctors were skilled in most aspects of medicine, including surgery.

Left: **Hippocrates made valuable contributions to early science and medicine. Part of his writings constitute a code of beliefs and conduct for physicians. Today, all medical students take as their pledge a version of that code, handed down through the centuries. With the so-called Hippocratic oath, doctors promise to respect life and to further science.**

Plato

Along with fellow Greek philosophers Socrates and Aristotle, Plato is widely considered one of the greatest thinkers of all time. Born into a prominent Athenian family in 428 B.C., Plato nursed political ambitions until he realized his stronger interests were philosophical. Building on the ideas of Socrates, Plato developed his own system of thought, which, in turn, inspired other philosophers, including the gifted Aristotle.

In about 387 B.C., Plato founded a philosophical and scientific institute called the Academy. Members of the Academy and Plato's friends achieved groundbreaking discoveries in biology, mathematics, and natural history. Plato delivered public lectures at the Academy and presented problems for its members to solve. He presided over the Academy until his death in 348 B.C.

The Greek Alphabet

Spoken for almost four thousand years, the Greek language is one of a group known as the Indo-European languages. Experts believe that the Indo-European languages developed from a single ancient form, because languages spoken from India to Eastern Europe share many common features. Greek, however, is somewhat unusual among these languages because it developed in relative isolation.

"Decoding" Ancient Symbols

Ancient Greeks carved their script on clay tablets, many of which survived for three thousand years or more. Much of what we understand about Greek script today is due to the efforts of Michael Ventris, an English cryptographer who treated the translation of the early symbols as a complicated code-breaking problem. A Minoan script discovered in about 1900 at the archaeological site of Knossos in Crete had baffled linguists and archaeologists for more than fifty years. In 1952, Ventris showed

Below: **Greek writing on fragments from the ruins of the Temple of Zeus at Olympia, in Peloponnesus, dates back to the early fifth century** B.C.

Greek letters	Corresponding English letters	Pronounced as in these words	Greek letters	Corresponding English letters	Pronounced as in these words
A α	A a	arm	N ν	N n	none
B β	V v	vase	Ξ ξ	X x	axe
Γ γ	G g	young	O o	O o	ox
Δ δ	D d	there	Π π	P p	pet
E ε	E e	egg	P ρ	R r	run
Z ζ	Z z	zoom	Σ σ	S s	sun
H η	I i	leave	T τ	T t	ten
Θ θ	Th th	thing	Υ υ	Y y	leave
I ι	I i	leave	Φ φ	F f	fun
K κ	K k	kind	X χ	Ch ch	look
Λ λ	L l	long	Ψ ψ	Ps ps	caps
M μ	M m	man	Ω ω	O o	ox

Above: **The twenty-four letters of the Greek alphabet are easily transliterated.**

the script to be the oldest known form of Greek, dating back more than three thousand years. When Ventris broke the code, he enabled historians to read all the fragments of Greek pottery that had been uncovered in archaeological digs. Linguists pieced together the history of modern Greek script. They now believe that modern Greek developed from earlier, simpler forms of writing in about the eighth century B.C., when ancient Greeks invented a script that included vowels. The Greek script continued to develop in two forms — one used in the eastern Greek islands and another used in western Greece — until 350 B.C. By then, the two forms had become quite similar, and the eastern, or Ionic, alphabet became the unofficial Greek standard. This same alphabet is used today. It has twenty-four letters, and each letter indicates a separate sound.

Other Alphabets

All the different alphabets of European languages today are derived directly or indirectly from Greek! In fact, the word *alphabet* itself comes from the first two letters of the Greek alphabet, *alpha* (AL-fah) and *beta* (VEE-tah). It first appeared in Latin, an offshoot of Greek, in the second or third century. The Cyrillic alphabet, used today by Serbs, Russians, Bulgarians, Ukrainians, and Belorussians, was invented in the ninth century by St. Cyril and St. Methodius, two Greek monks from Thessaloníki who brought Christianity to the southern Slavic people.

Names and Name Days

Greeks place great value on names, and many families follow a strict pattern to determine a new baby's name. The first boy is generally named after his paternal grandfather, while the eldest daughter receives her paternal grandmother's name. This custom acknowledges the mortality of the elderly relative but assures that he or she will live on through the child. In addition, of course, grandparents are thrilled to have a grandchild named after them. Sometimes, the custom is slightly altered. A man in a family with many children named after his father might do his wife's father the honor of naming an eldest

child after him. Alternatively, a woman trying to conceive might ask a saint for help, promising to name the child after the saint.

Above: **In Greece, baptism is a significant religious ritual. Baptismal names are usually the names of popular saints.**

Acquired Names

Generally, friends will give a Greek a nickname that describes some characteristic about him or her. These nicknames can become so established that sons and grandsons will inherit them, until, eventually, the original name fades from memory, and a new family name is born.

Marriage can affect a woman's name. In Greece, a married woman may choose to use a form of her husband's last name. For example, Papadopoulos' wife would be known as Mrs. Papadopoulou. The law also allows a married woman to keep her maiden name, if desired, and many do, especially those with careers in the public sector.

Celebrating Name Days

In Greece, only children celebrate their birthdays. The most important day of the year for an adult is his or her name day. Each saint in the Greek Orthodox Church is assigned a day in the church calendar. People celebrate the feast days of the saints after whom they are named.

Below: **A priest leads residents of Sérifos Island in a saint's day prayer.**

On the appointed day, friends visit or call to congratulate the person celebrating his or her name day. The host is expected to supply food and drinks. Unlike birthday parties in other countries, guests do not bring gifts. The merriment lasts the whole night as people move around from house to house, visiting in succession the friends who share that same name day.

Mortals are not the only ones for whom name days are celebrated. Each Greek town also has a patron saint and holds a huge celebration on that saint's day. Prayer meetings and processions honor the saint, and the whole town is festive.

Of Gods and Goddesses

Greece is home to perhaps the most famous gods and goddesses of all time. Myths developed as the ancient Greeks sought to explain the phenomena they observed in the world. The bolts of lightning they saw during thunderstorms became weapons cast by Zeus, father of the gods. Misfortune or bad luck was blamed on the wickedness of a mischievous god such as Pan. Gradually, a god or goddess was given dominion over his or her own sphere of influence, such as an element of nature or a valuable human trait. Poseidon, god of the sea, for example, received homage from fishermen and sailors. Before a battle, soldiers might ask Athena, goddess of warfare, wisdom, and justice, for victory. The gods and goddesses lived on Mt. Olympus and were organized in a pantheon, a heavenly collective, with Zeus at the head.

In the Image of Humans

The Greeks modeled their gods after themselves and imbued them with exaggerations of the characteristics, good and bad, they saw in themselves. Thus, Aphrodite's beauty was unrivaled in the universe; Hera's jealousy was unparalleled in all creation. Because the gods and goddesses were so human, their interactions with

Above: **In Greek mythology, Narcissus was an extraordinarily good-looking young man. When he rejected the love of Echo, a nymph, the angry gods made him fall in love with his own reflection in a spring. Narcissus pined away and died, and the flower that grew up in his place was named after him.**

Left: **A 1964 postage stamp featured Poseidon, the Greek god of the sea, who is usually depicted holding either a long-handled fish spear (as shown) or a trident, a three-pronged spear.**

each other resembled human relationships, giving rise to a huge collection of stories about these heavenly beings indulging in human follies and vices. At the same time, the Greeks felt at the mercy of their gods and goddesses. Greek legends told of people trying to do the best they could while the gods, with their own agendas, meddled in their affairs. In Homer's *Odyssey*, the Greek king Odysseus incurs the wrath of a goddess, who enlists the help of other deities to prevent him from ever reaching home after the war against Troy. Eventually, the aged hero returns home, but only with the help of an opposing faction of gods who take pity on his wretched plight.

The Gods Have Spoken

In ancient times, the Greeks believed the spirits of their gods inhabited certain shrines or temples known as oracles. By far the most famous ancient oracle, Apollo's Oracle at Delphi was consulted on matters of personal as well as political importance. Legend has it that a suggestion of the oracle led to the formation of the Olympic Games!

Above: **The medium who delivered Apollo's Oracle at Delphi was called a Pythia. After elaborate rituals of bathing and animal sacrifice, the Pythia would pronounce the oracle.**

ZEUS OR JUPITER?

Greek mythology was so well established and popular that when the Romans conquered Greece, they adopted Greek mythology, only changing the names of the gods and goddesses. Thus, the Greek god Zeus corresponds to the Roman god Jupiter, Hermes to Mercury, and Aphrodite to Venus.

Olives and Olive Oil

The ancient Greeks believed the olive was the gift of Athena, the Greek goddess of warfare, wisdom, and justice. As trade grew around the region, the Romans were quick to accept olives and start cultivating their own groves. Olives were first grown around the Mediterranean but have now spread elsewhere to countries with similar climates, such as Australia, New Zealand, and Central America. They were brought to America by Spanish missionaries. California is now an important producer of olives for the world olive market.

Olives first appear on trees in the spring. Over a number of months, they develop from tiny, gray berries with no seeds or oil into fleshy olives with oil. In the last stage before harvest, olives turn from green to reddish brown to black. Green olives are harvested between August and November, while black olives are left on the trees until March or even April to mature.

Below: **Large black nets cover the ground at harvest time in olive groves on Kérkira. Harvesters use long poles with containers attached to pick the olives, and the nets catch any stray olives that fall to the ground.**

The main difficulty in harvesting olives is that they have to be individually picked. Because these fruits are delicate and easily damaged by machines, olive plantations are usually small, family-run farms with little machinery.

A Healthy Type of Oil

Although experts advise us to cut down on fat in our diets, the human body needs some fat to be healthy. The trick is to consume the kinds of fats and oils that are healthiest for the body. Unlike saturated fats, such as butter and animal fats, olive oil is a monounsaturated fat, considered a "healthy" fat. Replacing regular cooking oil with olive oil lowers the amount of unhealthy cholesterol in the body, while increasing the good cholesterol necessary for healthy living. Surveys have shown that switching to olive oil could help prevent heart disease. Olive oil also prevents ulcers and gastritis by controlling acidity levels in the body. It is recommended for pregnant women, partly because it helps prevent loss of calcium. Finally, olive oil is easy for the system to digest and provides a large, quick energy boost.

Above: **In Greece, appetizers or side dishes may consist of olives and feta cheese, a variety of cheese made from goat's milk. Fresh olives are too bitter to be eaten. Processing takes the sharp edge off their taste.**

The Olympic Games

The most prestigious sporting event in the world today is the Olympic Games. Many athletes covet Olympic medals more than victory in any world championship.

The Beginning of a Tradition

The games began as part of a religious celebration in Olympia in the city-state of Elis, in northern Peloponnesus. Records of Olympic champions date back to 776 B.C., when there was only one contest, a footrace. In the following decades, other events were introduced, including boxing and chariot racing.

Before the Games, special messengers were sent off in every direction to announce the start of a sacred truce and the suspension of all disputes and warfare among the city-states. The victors of the Games were honored among all Greeks; their achievements were praised in memorials, poems, and songs.

Below: **Competitors in the 1896 Olympic Games in Athens line up for the start of the 100-meter race.**

Left: Greek actress Katerina Didaskalou, dressed in the robes of an ancient Greek priestess, lights the Olympic torch in Olympia, Greece. Runners carried the torch to Los Angeles in the United States, the host country of the 1984 Olympic Games.

In addition to inspiring succeeding generations to pursue competitive sports, the Games also contributed to a sense of unity between the Greek city-states, a contribution best measured by the fact that no wars were ever waged during the Games. The tradition of holding the Olympic Games every four years was abandoned in the fourth century A.D. as classical Greece declined.

The Modern Olympic Games

Frenchman Baron Pierre de Coubertin spearheaded the revival of the Olympic Games in 1896. Thirteen countries sent their best athletes to Athens to participate in forty-two sporting events. Gradually, the list of events grew, together with the prestige of winning. In 2004, to the great pride of Greeks, the Olympic Games will once again be hosted on Greek soil, in Athens.

An incredible ceremony opens the Olympic Games. With the Greek contingent in front and the host country bringing up the rear, all participants march around a huge stadium, pausing to take the Olympic oath in front of the flag of five interlocking rings. The opening ceremony ends with the arrival of a torch carried from Olympia, the original location of the games, and passed from runner to runner until it reaches the Olympic stadium of the host country. Once lit, the Olympic flame remains blazing until the games end and the flag is lowered.

MARATHON MAN

The 1896 Olympic Games introduced the first ever marathon, a long-distance footrace. A marathon commemorates the courageous deed of an Athenian soldier said to have run himself to death, in 490 B.C., carrying to Athens news of the Athenian victory over the Persians at the Battle of Marathon. Greek runner Spiros Louis was the first gold medalist in the modern Olympic marathon event. When Louis entered the Olympic stadium in Athens on the final leg of his race in 1896, he was greeted by rousing applause. So proud of him were the Greeks that Crown Prince Constantine and Prince George joined him on a circuit around the stadium.

63

The Parthenon

At the height of Athenian power in classical Greece, the statesman Pericles ordered the building of a complex, the Acropolis, on a hill in the center of Athens. At the heart of the complex was the Parthenon, a splendid monument dedicated to the goddess Athena, whom devotees called Athena Parthenos (Athena the Virgin).

In 447 B.C., Ictinus and Callicrates, the best architects in Athens, were ordered to start work on the temple. In 438 B.C., Phidias, the great Athenian sculptor, finished a magnificent three-story statue of Athena for the temple interior. The Parthenon, completed in 432 B.C., was a creation of supreme beauty. It was constructed of white marble, and its interior was lined with marble slabs intricately carved to show the procession of Panathenae, the most important festival in ancient Athens. Other walls showed more than three hundred men and women and various deities. The carving on the exterior eastern wall above the main entrance depicted Athena's birth, while the western wall showed the contest between Athena and Poseidon for possession of Athens. According to legend, Zeus had told Poseidon and Athena that he would give Athens to the one who brought him the most useful gift. Poseidon brought a horse, but Athena's winning gift was an olive tree, which became sacred in Athens.

The Parthenon, now in ruins, has seen the rise and fall of empires. Used as a temple in the fifth century, the monument became a church from the sixth to the fifteenth centuries, and a mosque during the Turkish occupation of Athens. In the seventeenth century, Venetians besieged the city, reducing the temple to ruins. In 1801, many of the Parthenon's marble carvings were removed and shipped to England by Lord Elgin. They are exhibited in the British Museum in London, and Greece is campaigning to have them returned to Athens.

Efforts to restore the Parthenon have been partly successful, but the monument now faces a new enemy — pollution. Exhaust fumes from the many vehicles in Athens mix with rain, forming acid rain, which corrodes the Parthenon's marble structure. Efforts are under way to protect this architectural treasure of the ancient world.

Above: **The Porch of the Caryatids has six statues for columns. It is part of a temple called the Eréchtheum, in Athens' Acropolis.**

Opposite: **The Parthenon stands on a hilltop overlooking the city of Athens. This ancient temple was dedicated to Athena, the patron saint of Athens and the Greek goddess of warfare, wisdom, and justice.**

Shadow Puppets

Greek shadow puppet theater, or *karaghiozis* (kah-RAH-gheeoh-zis), is a legacy of Turkish rule in Greece from the fourteenth to nineteenth centuries. Legend has it that this art form originated in Turkey in the fourteenth century, when a blacksmith angered the Turkish sultan by holding up construction of a mosque. The unfortunate blacksmith, named Karaghiozis, had such comical conversations with his mason friend that their colleagues stopped work to listen. The furious sultan punished the pair and had them sent away. Later, missing their clowning antics, he realized his mistake. To cheer up the sultan, courtiers cast shadows of puppets of the blacksmith and the mason onto a sheet and tried to recreate their comedy. The new art was called *karaghiozis* in the blacksmith's honor.

Over centuries, karaghiozis has evolved into a complicated skill that takes years to master. A modern performance uses flat

WHERE DID KARAGHIOZIS ORIGINATE?

Some believe karaghiozis was created by members of the Turkish sultan's court in the fourteenth century. Historians prefer another explanation. They believe the technique began in Indonesia and came to Greece via a trade route through China, India, and Turkey.

Left: **A shadow puppet craftsman paints part of his next creation. A completed puppet is displayed on the door of his studio, or workshop.**

puppets made of painted leather and plastic. Hinged at their joints, the puppets are manipulated with sticks. A light source casts the shadows of the puppets onto a hanging cloth. The audience watches from the other side of the cloth, seeing only the shadows. The skill of such a performance lies with the puppeteer, who sometimes works alone, an incredible task given the variety of voices, noises, and instruments needed for a production. Karaghiozis is an endangered art that is shrinking as television and the movies steal its audience. Today, very few puppeteers perform, and only a handful have young apprentices.

Above: **An experienced puppeteer passes on his secrets to his young apprentices. As demanding for the puppeteer as it is entertaining for the audience, karaghiozis is now a dying art.**

The Story of Karaghiozis

The main character in the performance, the blacksmith Karaghiozis, is usually portrayed as a short man with little hair. He is often down on his luck, barefoot, and dressed in rags. Most plays are hugely comical affairs revolving around his attempts to support himself and his family. Karaghiozis tries to make money by impersonating prominent persons, but luck is never quite on his side. The stories generally close with the misguided hero's capture and an occasional beating before he is thrown into jail. "Oh Mother, look what has happened!" is his usual closing lament.

Sweet Treats

Greeks have elevated the art of baking to perfection. The local sweet shop, or *zacharoplasteion* (zaa-haa-ropla-STEEON), sells the most mouthwatering variety of delights.

A Scrumptious Experience

A sweet shop in Greece is more than simply an eating place — it is pure heaven for anyone with a sweet tooth. The aroma of almonds, fresh pastry, and fruit waft from the delicate, glazed shapes in the shop window. Inside the shop, customers sit and enjoy a stunning range of desserts, from *kadaifi* (ka-DAEE-fee) (almond-filled pastry soaked in honey) to profiteroles. Greek profiteroles are tasty sponge cakes soaked in syrup and liqueur and covered with custard and cream.

Perhaps the most popular of all Greek desserts is *baklava* (baa-klaa-VAA), which comes in several varieties. The most famous is a heavily spiced creation of walnuts, found on Thásos.

Below: **A food vendor in Athens displays a tempting array of donuts, pretzels, and breads.**

Left: **Kadaifi and baklava are among the most popular Greek desserts.**

Filled with egg custard and flavored with orange flower water and cinnamon, the pastry version is also delicious. The semolina sponge cake soaked in cognac and orange syrup satisfies the most demanding palate.

Halva (haal-VA), another famous dessert, is available from street markets. It is usually sliced from huge loaves dotted with pistachios and almonds. Again, every region has its own variety. The halva from Smyrna comes in large, circular flat blocks that are grainy and yellowish in color; the version from Thessaly has a texture more like gelatin and resembles Turkish delight. Chocolate fans love the variety streaked with chocolate. Greeks eat this popular treat with a sprinkling of lemon juice and cinnamon.

Homemade Desserts

After a meal in a Greek home, guests are traditionally offered a piece of fruit preserved in syrup. Almost any fruit or vegetable can be preserved this way. Yet another favorite dessert is the "submarine," a spoonful of vanilla-flavored cream dissolved in a glass of iced water to create an exquisitely perfumed drink.

The Women of Greece

In the past, the traditional Greek view of a woman's role in society was very conservative. Girls learned to sew and embroider at a young age, and the pride of the household rested in the women's skills at needlework and home economics. Today, this view has changed in all except the most conservative, isolated villages. While public life in Greece remains dominated by men, the 1975 constitution strictly safeguards the equality of men and women, and many laws have been enacted since 1981 to improve the status of women. In July 1985, the General Secretariat of Equality of the Prime Minister's Office was established, with the task of cooperating with all ministries in implementing the principles of equality.

The Modern Woman

In recent years, women's rights have progressed greatly. A career has become important to many women, and earning a good

Below: **A Kárpathian woman stands proudly in front of her needle-work creations in a home filled with hand-painted plates, framed photographs, and other decorative touches.**

Left: **A policewoman directs traffic on a busy street in Athens. Careers are becoming increasingly important to many Greek women. Women now constitute about 35 percent of the work force in Greece.**

income has become a priority. Assertiveness and action are the new feminine values, but this does not mean that women no longer treasure their family ties. The family unit still endures, and many families now support and encourage women's education.

With the reform of the Family Code, the patriarchal nature of the traditional family unit has been abolished. Husbands and wives must make joint decisions on any matter concerning their lives. In the early 1980s, the government abolished the dowry system, an old institution whereby the father or relatives of the bride gave the groom sums of money or property to alleviate the burden of marriage. Recent legislation has tried to remove the final vestiges of discrimination in education and has definitively abolished the separation of professions into "male" and "female."

With increased responsibility at the workplace and women occupying more visible positions in companies and even government, traditional attitudes are rapidly giving way to equality between the sexes, and many men are being forced to reassess their conservative views.

Zákinthos and More

The word *ecology* comes from the Greek word *oikos* (OY-koss), meaning "house," and the science of ecology concerns how animals interact with their environment. Modern Greece takes a strong interest in ecology because its land is so closely intertwined with its economy. Tourists are attracted by the natural beauty of the Greek islands. Since Greece depends on the sea for some of its food, clean oceans are in the country's interest. Ecologists in Greece concentrate on the compromise between developing the economy and caring for the countryside.

Zákinthos

Greece is doing its part to preserve endangered species. The conservation project on Zákinthos is especially significant because this small Greek island is the most important egg-laying site in the Mediterranean for rare loggerhead sea turtles. These gentle giants can weigh up to 350 pounds (159 kilograms). Although they spend most of their time in the sea, they come ashore to lay their eggs. The Zákinthos project aims to keep their environment free from pollution and to protect the turtles and their eggs from poachers.

Left: **The loggerhead turtle is an endangered animal that Greek environmentalists are doing their best to save.**

Underwater World

Part of a European Union initiative to study the Mediterranean, the Mediterranean Targeted Project involves a tiny submarine called *Jago*, designed to plumb the depths of the sea. With 9,300 miles (14,970 km) of coast, Greece has been an active member of the group in the eastern Mediterranean. The project's marine biologists have discovered many fascinating new species of fish. They are also trying to regulate fishing so Greece's once-abundant fishing grounds can replenish themselves.

Protecting the Hunted

Hunting has traditionally been practiced since ancient times and is often mentioned in myths. As forests disappear, sport hunting is an increasing threat to many species of wildlife, including deer, small game, and wild fowl. In an effort to discourage hunting and protect endangered species, the Greek government has established several national parks where hunting is forbidden.

Above: **Fishermen on the island of Zákinthos sell fish from their boat. In recent years, the Greek government has tightened its laws on fishing to ensure the recovery of Greece's fishing grounds.**

RELATIONS WITH NORTH AMERICA

The founding fathers of the United States turned to classical Greek philosophy for guidance in shaping the nation. They discovered in the writings of Plato and Aristotle the ideals of democracy and individual rights, values upheld by the U.S. Constitution.

Formal relations between Greece and North America began relatively recently, in the twentieth century, and weathered decades of uncertainty and suspicion in the 1950s and 1960s to

Opposite: **Beach resorts on the island of Poros draw hundreds of American tourists to Greece each year.**

Below: **A Greek-American in Florida performs a dance in traditional dress.**

arrive at today's warm accord. U.S.-Greek ties have been strengthened by trade agreements and good relations between the leaders of both countries.

There is a healthy respect between the peoples of Greece and North America. Just as North American culture, from fashion to film, fascinates Greeks, the United States and Canada also bear the stamp of Greek influence, from food to architecture. More than three million Greek immigrants now live in the United States and Canada, and famous Americans such as Michael Dukakis, Pete Sampras, and Jennifer Aniston trace their ancestry to Greece.

Fighting Communism

American involvement in the politics of Greece was largely motivated by a fear of communism and by the way the Soviet Union was gaining influence in Europe. After Greece fell to Germany in 1941, Greek resistance groups were organized in the hills to harass the German occupying forces. The first resistance group formed was the communist National Liberation Front (EAM). Its military arm was known by the initials ELAS. Widespread local support for EAM/ELAS alarmed the U.S. government. Moreover, many non-communist Greeks supported the movement, simply because it was the first resistance group formed.

After World War II, the British helped reinstall the monarchy in Greece, frustrating EAM's wish to form a communist

THE TRUMAN DOCTRINE

On March 12, 1947, U.S. President Harry S. Truman (*left*), determined to combat the spread of communism in the Mediterranean, granted immediate financial aid to Greece and Turkey. Congress issued $400 million in compliance with the president's policy, which became known as the Truman Doctrine.

Left: **Communist guerillas captured by the Greek government in 1947 await the carrying out of their death sentence by shooting. The government defeated the communist guerilla movement in 1949, after many years of fighting.**

government. Feeling that they had not received their just reward after fighting so hard, the communists took to the hills again, this time in rebellion against the struggling monarchy.

In need of foreign assistance in the form of money and arms, the Greek government appealed to the United States for help. U.S. President Harry S. Truman, fearing the growing Soviet influence in Eastern Europe, granted financial support for anti-communist efforts in Turkey and Greece in what became known as the Truman Doctrine. The Greek communist rebels were defeated in 1949. The legacy of this civil war was a strong right-wing, or conservative, anti-communist government that was careless about civil rights and brutal in quashing dissent.

NATO

In 1952, Greece joined the North Atlantic Treaty Organization (NATO), a group of nations committed to fighting the spread of communism. Membership in NATO ensured the continuation of U.S. aid to Greece, but it also resulted in an American influence on Greek politics that many liberal Greeks found troublesome.

Road to Democracy

In 1964, tired of the power struggles after World War II, the Greek people voted the Center Union Party, led by George Papandreou, into power. The party promised reform and modernization, but their changes were met with strong opposition. The political instability that followed provided an opportunity for the military, led by Colonel George Papadopoulos, to take over the country in 1967. Ironically, the military acted out a NATO contingency plan in its seizure of power. Riding on the back of U.S. efforts to combat communism, the Greek military used American money, planning, and technology to subvert democracy in Greece for seven years.

The collapse of the military dictatorship restored democracy to Greece in 1974. The people's uneasiness about U.S. support for the military junta played an important part in electoral campaigns. Andreas Papandreou's Panhellenic Socialist Movement (PASOK) swept to power on a platform promising resignation from NATO and the removal of U.S. military bases from Greece. Once in power, however, the party's policies proved

Below: **Colonel George Papadopoulos, regent of Greece in 1967, addresses the Greek "parliament." During the rule of the colonels, there was no elected parliament. The officials shown here are members of the appointed cabinet, heads of the armed forces, rectors of universities, and legal advisors to the cabinet. Democracy did not return to Greece until 1974.**

Left: **In 1996, Greek President Konstantinos Stephanopoulos (*right*) met with U.S. President Bill Clinton (*left*) to discuss the Cyprus issue and economic relations between Greece and the United States. Ties between these countries have steadily improved with the growth of the Greek immigrant community in the United States.**

moderate, and leases on the American military bases were renewed. This tactic of aggressive election rhetoric, followed by moderate policies, proved a winning formula in a few elections, satisfying both Greeks and American interests in Greece.

Strengthening Ties

In 1990, the United States and Greece signed a Mutual Defense and Cooperation Agreement to regulate defense relations between the two countries. Both countries also cooperated in the international fight against terrorism and drugs. When Iraq invaded Kuwait in 1991, the United States spearheaded efforts to liberate Kuwait. Greece became a key player in the Gulf War. Its airbases were a vital link in the victory over Iraq. Greece and the United States are also members of the Partnership for Peace initiative (PFP). In 1995, as part of its PFP efforts, Greece organized a multinational civil defense exercise in the Balkans. In the scenario, the United States, Greece, and three Balkan nations joined forces to render aid to earthquake victims in the region.

With the end of the Cold War, the period of nonviolent animosity between the United States and the U.S.S.R., Greece nurses new hopes that the United States might redirect its considerable influence to Turkey and reduce tensions in the Mediterranean, especially over Cyprus.

Emigration

An exodus took place in 1911 when prices of farm produce fell in world markets. This slump hit Greek farmers very badly, and many left their farms, moving first to major Greek cities and then on to North America and Europe in search of better lives. Another wave of emigration occurred in the aftermath of World War II. Greece had been ravaged by Italy and Germany and lacked the resources to feed its population. Again, the United States and Canada were the most common destinations.

More recently, free movement within the European Union has enabled Greeks with specialized interests to pursue jobs in other European countries. Improved standards of living in Greece, however, are drawing back many Greeks who studied and made careers abroad.

Left: This second-generation Greek-American attends college in Detroit, Michigan. Many Greeks settled in North America after the two world wars and eventually became American or Canadian citizens, raising families in their new homelands.

New Homes

Between two and three million Greek-Americans have made the United States their home. New York City and Chicago claim the largest enclaves of Greeks living outside of Greece.

First-generation Greek-Americans readily speak and write Greek. Among subsequent generations, however, many young Greek-Americans, conscious of integrating into the American community, understand the language but are reluctant to speak it outside their families. Their commitment to education, hard work, and family values has allowed them to prosper in their new home.

Both the U.S. and Greek governments recognize the need to strengthen cultural ties between the two countries. To this end, in 1996, a two-way communications agreement was signed. The agreement offers Greek-Americans the opportunity to receive, in the United States, programs broadcast in Greece.

The Greek-Canadian community in Canada numbers about three hundred thousand. Toronto is one of the most popular destinations for immigrant Greeks. The Greek population is so well settled there that a section of the city is affectionately called "Little Greece."

Above: **Greek tavérnas, diners, and delicatessens are a common sight in many North American cities, reflecting the popularity of Greek food.**

Above: **American tourists visit the ruins of Delphi.**

Americans in Greece

Social and economic ties between Greece and the United States remain strong. American businesses operate in Greece, and more than 80,000 Americans live there — so many that the American International School of Athens was set up to cater to the needs of American children growing up in Athens. Many Americans of Greek descent still have relatives living in Greece, to whom they pay regular visits. Life in Greece can be far more relaxing than in North America, and many Greek-Americans choose to return to Greece for holidays.

Tourism

Tourism is a cornerstone of the Greek economy, and, every year, hundreds of Americans flock to the sunny islands and sandy beaches of Greece. The tremendous historical and cultural heritage also draws visitors from all over the world — 12 million in 1998. Many Americans have a romantic attachment to the "birthplace of Western civilization." For them, a pilgrimage to the beauty of Greece's ancient monuments is a must on any European trip.

TRADE AND BUSINESS

The United States and Greece have a close connection through trade. Greek olive oil is gaining popularity in the United States. In fact, it is considered a superior product and commands a higher price than the U.S. equivalent.

Greeks in North America

Life in the Greek communities of North America continues much as it does in Greece. Greek national and religious celebrations are faithfully observed and thoroughly enjoyed. Mouthwatering Greek cuisine has made Greek diners and restaurants famous throughout North American cities.

Several Greek or Greek-American celebrities have found success in the United States. Greek shipping tycoon and businessman Aristotle Onassis was born in Smyrna when the city still belonged to Greece. When it was captured by the Turks in 1922, Onassis and his family fled to Greece. Onassis later set up a tobacco business in Argentina that expanded to include trading and shipping.

Greek-American operatic soprano Maria Callas was born Maria Kalogeropoulos in New York in 1923. In 1937, she left the United States to study at the Athens Conservatory in Greece. International concert appearances followed her graduation, and she also made a brief foray into films. Callas died in 1977.

Above: **Born in California and raised in New York, popular American television and movie star Jennifer Aniston has Greek ancestry.**

Left: **In 1968, Greek shipping tycoon Aristotle Onassis married Jacqueline Bouvier Kennedy, the widow of assassinated U.S. President John F. Kennedy. By the time of Onassis's death in 1975, his fleet of merchant ships was among the largest in the world.**

Orthodox Christianity in North America

Greek immigrants to North America brought their religion with them. The first Greek Orthodox church in the United States was built in New Orleans in 1864. As Greek immigration to North America increased in the early twentieth century, new churches sprang up. By 1916, there were fifty-nine Greek Orthodox churches in the United States.

In 1922, Meletios Metaxakis, the Ecumenical Patriarch of the Greek Orthodox Church in Istanbul (formerly Constantinople), established a Greek archdiocese in North America. Since then, four archbishops have led the Greek Orthodox Archdiocese of North and South America through many important changes, setting up a school of theology, allowing the preaching of sermons in English, and establishing the Greek Orthodox religion as one of the major faiths in the United States. Elected in 1996, the fourth and current Archbishop of America is Metropolitan Spyridon.

Below: **The distinct domes of an Orthodox church in Pittsburgh, Pennsylvania, stand out from the rest of the city skyline.**

Athens of the South

The admiration many Americans have for Greek culture is perhaps nowhere more evident than in Nashville, Tennessee, where there is a replica of the Parthenon. The structure was built in 1897 for the Tennessee Centennial Exposition. The idea was to underline the state capital's reputation as the Athens of the South, but the replica, accurate to one-eighth of an inch, proved so popular it was left as a permanent exhibit.

The building deteriorated gradually and had to be completely rebuilt using concrete in 1931. The central piece of the building is a gigantic statue of Athena. The architects responsible for the renovations were Russell E. Hart and William B. Dinsmoor, who was also an archaeologist. They traveled to Greece many times to see the original Parthenon and modeled their building after it as closely as possible. Most experts acknowledge that Hart and Dinsmoor did a commendable job.

Today, the Parthenon replica stands proudly in Centennial Park in Nashville. Some of its external details have required minor restoration since Hart and Dinsmoor's work. Residents joke good humoredly that it is the perfect image of its original — right down to the crumbling details!

Above: **A replica of the Parthenon in Nashville, Tennessee, is an accurate likeness of the original in Athens, Greece.**

OLD WORLD LEGACY

Many cities and towns in North America take their names from ancient Greek city-states, including Athens, Georgia; Corinth, Mississippi; and Sparta, Wisconsin.

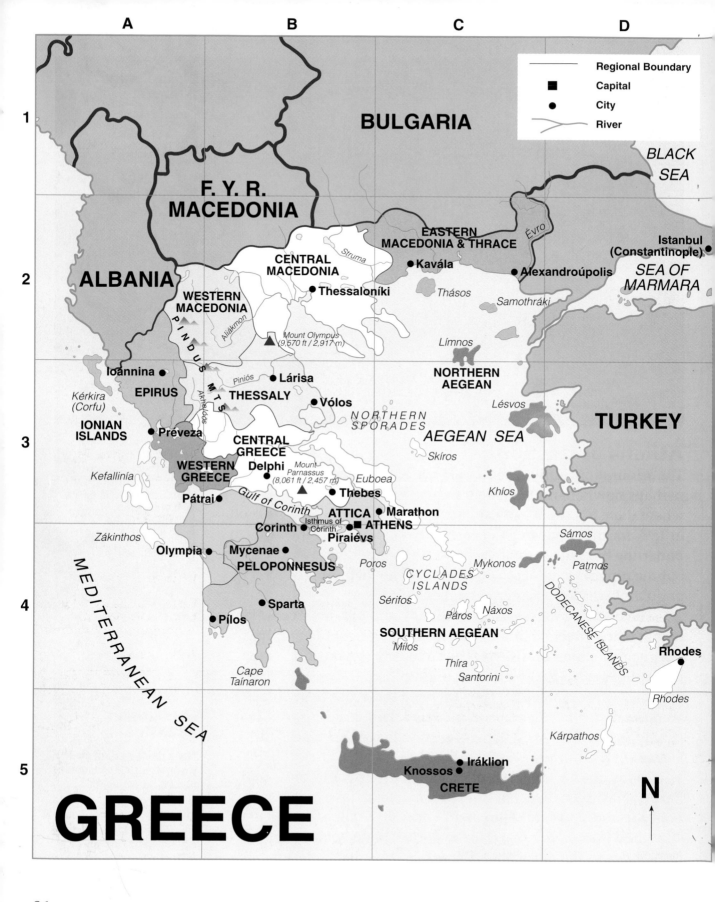

GREECE

Above: A crater lake on one of the Santorini islands.

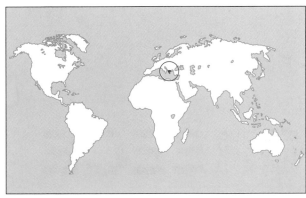

GREECE

N

Above: **The islands of Santorini offer spectacular sunset views.**

How Is Your Geography?

Learning to identify the main geographical areas and points of a country can be challenging. Although it may seem difficult at first to memorize the locations and spellings of major cities or the names of mountain ranges, rivers, deserts, lakes, and other prominent physical features, the end result of this effort can be very rewarding. Places you previously did not know existed will suddenly come to life when referred to in world news, whether in newspapers, television reports, or other books and reference sources. This knowledge will make you feel a bit closer to the rest of the world, with its fascinating variety of cultures and physical geography.

For use in a classroom setting, the instructor can make duplicates of this map using a copy machine. (PLEASE DO NOT WRITE IN THIS BOOK!) Students can then fill in any requested information on their individual map copies. For use one-on-one, the student can also make copies of the map on a copy machine and use them as a study tool. The student can practice identifying place names and geographical features on his or her own.

Greece at a Glance

Official Name	The Hellenic Republic
Capital	Athens
Official Language	Greek
Population	10,565,000 (1998 estimate)
Land Area	50,949 square miles (131,958 square km)
Regions	Attica, Central Greece, Central Macedonia, Crete, Eastern Macedonia and Thrace, Epirus, Ionian Islands, Northern Aegean, Peloponnesus, Southern Aegean, Thessaly, Western Greece, Western Macedonia
Highest Point	Mount Olympus (9,570 feet/2,917 m)
Major Rivers	Aliákmon
	Akhelöós
	Piniós
Official Religion	Greek Orthodox Christianity
Famous Leaders	Alexander the Great
	Eleuthérios Venizélos
	Constantine Karamanlis
	Andreas Papandreou
Important Holidays	Pascha, or Easter
	Independence Day
	Ochi Day
Flag	Nine alternating blue and white horizontal stripes with a white cross on a blue background in the upper left corner. The cross represents Greek Orthodox Christianity. Blue and white are the national colors of Greece.
Currency	Drachma (Grd 280 = U.S. $1 as of 1999)

Opposite: **Petros the pelican is the mascot of the island of Mykonos, Greece.**

Glossary

Greek Vocabulary

alpha (AL-fah): the first letter of the Greek alphabet.

baklava (baa-klaa-VAA): a Greek walnut dessert or pastry with layers of dough filled with ground nuts.

beta (VEE-tah): the second letter of the Greek alphabet.

dimotiki (dee-moh-tee-KEE): demotic Greek, a commonly spoken form of the Greek language.

ekklesia (ek-KLEE-see-ah): a popular assembly or gathering of debaters in classical Athens; church.

gymnasium (jim-NAH-see-um): a secondary school for young people aged thirteen to fifteen.

halva (haal-VA): a dessert made chiefly with ground nuts and honey; halva comes in many varieties.

kadaifi (ka-DAEE-fee): an almond-filled pastry soaked in honey.

kafedaki (kah-fay-DHAH-kee): a rich, finely ground coffee popular in Greece.

kalamari (ka-lah-MAH-ree): squid.

karaghiozis (kah-RAH-gheeoh-zis): shadow puppet theater.

katharévousa (kah-thah-REH-voo-sah): "pure" Greek, a form of the Greek that is much closer to the ancient language than dimotiki.

lyceum (lee-SEE-um): in the Greek education system, an institution students attend from age sixteen.

nonos (noh-NOS): godparent.

ochi (o-HEE): no.

oikos (OY-koss): a house.

ouzo (OO-zoh): a clear liquor with anise and licorice flavor. It is distilled from the residue of grapes after wine is made.

Pascha (PAHS-kah): Easter.

podosphero (poh-DOHS-fay-roh): soccer.

polis (POH-lis): a Greek city-state in the classical period; a small country centered around the city for which it was named.

retsina (ret-SEE-nah): a Greek wine flavored with resin.

souvlaki (soov-LAH-kee): skewered pieces of lamb cooked on a grill or barbecued.

tavérna (tah-VER-nah): a Greek restaurant.

vouli (VOO-li): the Greek parliament.

zacharoplasteion (zaa-haa-ropla-STEEON): a sweet shop.

English Vocabulary

acoustics: the characteristics of a room, hall, stadium, or theater that determine the quality of sounds in it.

Balkans: the territories of Yugoslavia, Romania, Bulgaria, Albania, Greece, and the European part of Turkey.

bauxite: a clay-like rock consisting of aluminum compounds mixed with impurities.

Byzantine Empire: the eastern half of the Roman Empire, which split in two in A.D. 285. The empire is named after its capital, Byzantium, later renamed Constantinople (now Istanbul, Turkey).

cryptic: puzzling.

cryptographer: an expert in the study of secret writing or symbols.

demotic: relating to the ordinary, everyday form of a language.

garrison: a military post.

guerillas: soldiers who use surprise attacks, raids, and other tactics in enemy-held territory.

Hippocratic oath: a pledge to respect life and work for scientific progress. Named after Hippocrates, the ancient Greek physician, the oath is taken today by those entering the medical profession.

idiom: a style of language particular to a certain region or group of people.

isthmus: a narrow strip of land connecting two larger landmasses.

junta: the government formed by the military in Greece after the 1967 coup; a small group ruling a country, especially after a coup and before a legal government has been instituted.

liqueur: a strong, sweet, alcoholic drink.

lobbyists: people who try to influence legislation or public opinion for a special cause.

monounsaturated fat: a kind of fat associated with a low cholesterol content and generally regarded as healthy.

natural selection: the process of nature by which life-forms adapted to certain environmental conditions tend to survive, reproduce, and pass on their traits, while those less well adapted tend to die off.

nomadic: relating to people who have no permanent homes and move from place to place, usually along a traditional route, in search of food or pasture.

oracle: a shrine or temple at which requests are made to a deity and divine answers conveyed through a medium or priest.

oratory: the art of public speaking, especially in a formal, eloquent way.

pantheon: the deities of a particular mythology considered as a group.

perspective: the technique of depicting spatial relationships on a flat surface.

prestigious: having a favorable reputation arising from success, achievement, rank, or other desirable qualities.

referenda: the practice of voting on matters proposed by a legislative body or political interest group.

Renaissance: the period of artistic, literary, and academic revival in Europe beginning in the fourteenth century and extending to the seventeenth.

replenish: to make full or complete again.

rhetoric: the art of effectively using language in speech or writing.

sanctuaries: places of safety and protection.

staunch: firm, steadfast, or loyal.

synod: an assembly of church delegates that decides church matters.

terra cotta: a hard, brownish red, fired clay used for pottery, sculpture, and architectural ornaments.

thyme: any plant in the mint family; an herb with narrow, aromatic leaves used for seasoning.

transliteration: changing the words and letters of one language into corresponding characters of another language.

welded tuff: a rock formation of solidified magma from a volcanic eruption.

More Books to Read

Across the Aegean: An Artist's Journey from Athens to Istanbul. Marlene McLoughlin (Chronicle Books)

Ancient Greece. Judith Simpson (Time-Life Books)

Athens. Cities of the World series. Conrad Stein (Children's Press)

First Facts about the Ancient Greeks. Fiona MacDonald (Peter Bedrick)

Greece. Cultures of the World series. Jill DuBois (Marshall Cavendish)

Greece. Festivals of the World series. Efstathia Sioras (Gareth Stevens)

Greek Americans. Cultures of America series. David Phillips and Steven Ferry (Benchmark Books)

Greek and Roman Science. World History series. Don Nardo (Lucent Books)

The Greek News. Anton Powell and Phillip Steele (Candlewick)

Greek People. Robert B. Kebric (Mayfield)

Mediterranean Cats. Hans Silvester (Chronicle Books)

The Parthenon. Great Buildings series. Peter Chrisp (Raintree/Steck Vaughn)

Videos

Ancient Splendors. (Reader's Digest Video)

Fodor's Video Greece. (TravelWorld Video and J. Mitchell Johnson)

Greece: Playground of the Gods. (International Video Network)

Web Sites

www.greekembassy.org/

www.athens2004.gr

www.areianet.gr/infoxenios

www.ariadne-t.gr

Due to the dynamic nature of the Internet, some web sites stay current longer than others. To find additional web sites, use a reliable search engine with one or more of the following keywords to help you locate information about Greece. Keywords: *Alexander the Great, Athens, Cyprus, Greek-Americans, Olympic Games, Parthenon, Zákinthos.*

Index